The Ebony Book of

Black Achievement

by Margaret Peters

Designed and illustrated
by Cecil L. Ferguson

New Revised Edition

Johnson Publishing Company Inc.

Chicago, Ill. 1974

Contents

Mansa Musa

? -1337

Mansa Musa

H E RULED an empire as large as Western Europe. He made an impressive pilgrimage, accompanied by a retinue esti- mated at 60,000 men, carrying over two thousand pounds of gold. He ascended to his ivory throne preceded by musicians playing upon gold and silver instruments. The monarch so described was not an oriental potentate or a European from the age of chivalry. He was Mansa Musa, famed African ruler of Mali, the powerful Sudanese empire.

These Sudanese empires (Ghana, Mali, and Songhay) have been widely praised by writers such as Al-Bakri (eleventh century), Ibn Batuta (fourteenth century) and Leo Africanus (sixteenth century). These men wrote about the wealth and pomp of the Sudanese empires, but they also described the fine houses and buildings, the love of justice, the political and military ability of the rulers, and the fine scholarship at Timbuktu. Benedetto Dei, a Florentine merchant, described the stone palace, court life, and university of Timbuktu in 1470, more than twenty years before the so-called New World was accidentally discovered. More recently, English historian Basil Davidson noted that next to eleventh century Ghana, Anglo-Saxon England must have seemed a lowly, poor place.

Ghana had become dominant, partly because its location enabled it to control the vast gold-salt trade and partly because of its people's skill in smelting iron. As Ghana declined, following an Almoravid invasion, numerous small wars finally resulted in the seizure of power by Sumanguru. In 1230 (some authors say 1240), Sumanguru was defeated by the legendary Sundiati Keita, founder of the empire of Mali. Mali, controlling the gold-salt trade, became more powerful than Ghana had been, just as Songhay later would be even stronger.

Mansa Musa, a descendant of Sundiati, ruled from 1312 to 1337, at one time as Mansa (Emperor) over as many as twenty-four regions of Africa. His territory extended to southern cities like Walata, the salt deposits of Taghaza to the north, the lands of the Fulani to the west, and the important trading centers of Timbuktu and Gao.

Mansa Musa is remembered not only as an excellent administrator and military leader, but also as a most devout Moslem and a patron of fine architecture. As a Moslem, it was his duty to make a pilgrimage to the holy city of Mecca. Well supplied with food, gold, and extra clothing (woven from cotton grown in his own kingdom), Musa set out across the Sahara, the largest desert region on earth. He stopped in Cairo, where he met and favorably impressed the Sultan of Egypt with his aristocratic demeanor and his generosity in distributing large quantities of gold. The Sultan honored the distinguished Mansa by presenting him with many gifts of horses, camels, and clothing.

When Mansa arrived in Mecca, he performed the ceremonies of the pilgrimage and received the title Haji (one who has made the Hajj or pilgrimage). He stayed there for several months, and when he began the journey back to Mali, Es-Saheli, the noted Arabian architect, traveled with him. Es-Saheli's influence was soon evident in some of the many beautiful buildings for which Mali was famous. The auditorium in the capital city of Niani, the palace in the fabulous city of Timbuktu, and the mosque in Gao are typical of the architectural advances made during the reign of this enlightened ruler.

The talents of Mansa Musa were many, but the greatness of Mali was not based entirely on his ability. After his death in 1337, Mali continued to be an exemplary empire. The Africans of Mali were highly praised for their honesty. Ibn Batuta, a scholar from Tangier who lived in the kingdom for one year in 1352, wrote about his experiences in Mali. He praised the Africans for their hatred of injustice and for the great degree of safety enjoyed by travelers, who had no reason to fear robbers.

Mali was thus an important part of Africa more than 250 years before the English settled Jamestown. It was a continent with its own cultures, skilled craftsmen, monetary systems, well-developed graphic arts, varied political and social institutions, and capable rulers.

Estevanico

ca. 1500-1537

Estevanico

T OO OFTEN it is stated that the first Africans arrived in the present-day United States. In fact, blacks were helping build up the so-called New World over one hundred years before the Pilgrims landed at Plymouth. Blacks worked with Ponce de Leon in Florida in 1513 and in 1565 helped build St. Augustine, which became the first permanent settlement in the present United States. Blacks staged a successful slave rebellion in the Spanish settlement near the Pedee River in 1526.

In Latin America, which Hubert Herring says should logically be called Indo-Afro-Ibero-America, blacks were with Balboa when the Pacific was sighted in 1513. They helped build the first path across the Isthmus. Four years later, one of the blacks with Cortez planted the first wheat crop in Mexico, while others helped build aqueducts which are still in use. Blacks in Peru, in addition to working in the fields, guarded the precious olive trees which had been brought in by Antonio de Rivera in 1560.

Unfortunately, the names of most of these blacks are unknown. However, the exploits of one individual were recorded. That man strode onto the stage of history in 1528. This explorer was Estevanico, or little Stephen. Estevanico was the chief scout of an expedition of three hundred persons led by Panfilio de Nervaez. The expedition party reached Florida in 1528, intending both to conquer the Indians

9

and to establish a Spanish colony. Neither goal was attained. Nervaez was drowned and only fifteen of the three hundred survived a hurricane.

The survivors, including Estevanico and Cabeza de Vaca, treasurer of the expedition, began the long and dangerous trek to the Spanish settlement in Mexico City. Only four of them finished the journey, which took eight years. De Vaca wrote about the hazards they had faced in his book *The Journey of Alvar Nunez Cabeza de Vaca,* in which he gave Estevanico credit for having saved his life. De Vaca's book helped inspire the later explorations of Coronado and DeSoto, and in this way the influence of Estevanico was far-reaching.

During this long journey of exploration Estevanico became familiar with the geography of the country and with several Indian dialects. He was highly respected by the Indians because of the knowledge of medicine he had acquired from the Moors. Estevanico was therefore chosen by the viceroy of Mexico to guide an expedition in search of the Seven Cities of Cibola, legendary wealthy cities which were supposed to exist in what is now the southwestern United States.

When Fray Marcos, the leader of the expedition, fell ill, Estevanico and four Indians continued the journey alone. Estevanico sent back wooden crosses of various sizes to the priest to show the size of the settlements they found. One cross was as large as a man, indicating a very large settlement (probably one of the Zuni villages). A few days after this cross arrived two Indian guides returned, wounded, to Fray Marcos's camp. They told the priest that Estevanico had been imprisoned, and probably killed, at a city where his peace offers had been refused. The legendary cities were never found but Estevanico, the black explorer, became the first person to explore the territory that is now New Mexico and Arizona.

Crispus Attucks

1723-1770

Crispus Attucks

I N BOSTON, Massachusetts on the evening of March 5, 1770, British soldiers fired their muskets at point-blank range into a crowd of protesters, led by "a stout man with a long stick." The "stout man," later identified by an eyewitness as "the molatto (sic)," Crispus Attucks, was the first to fall, "killed on the spot with two balls entering his breast." This event, later known as the Boston Massacre, was the culmination of the resentment and outrage felt by the citizens of Boston as a result of soldiers being quartered on their property by order of the King, to enforce laws passed in England without their consent. The most despised of these laws was The Stamp Act, (1765) and later, the tax on tea, (1773) which resulted in the "Boston Tea Party."

John Adams, later the second president of the United States, stated at the trial of the soldiers for the deaths of Attucks and the four others, Samuel Gray, Samuel Maverick, James Caldwell and Patrick Carr, that "This Attucks appeared to have undertaken to be the hero of the night; and to lead the army . . . to form them in the first place in Dock Square, and march them up King Street (now State Street) with their clubs . . ." The five men killed that night were buried together in a common grave, and Crispus Attucks, who, with his cordwood stick had raised his arm against the soldiers of King George III, became the first martyr of the American Revolution.

Twenty years earlier, Crispus Attucks had escaped from slavery and taken to sea. His owner, William Brown of Framingham, Mass., advertised for the runaway in the *Boston Gazette,* March 2, 1750. The advertisement describes Crispus as being "about 6 ft. 2 inches tall, with short curled hair and knees closer together than common." He was about 27 years of age when he made his escape to freedom. During the nearly twenty years that passed between September 30, 1750 and March 5, 1770, "Attucks, who was born in Framingham," had considered New Providence in the Bahamas, his home; apparently working as a seaman on ships which ran between the West Indies and the New England ports. He and his fellow martyrs had come from Dock Street and the Harbor to the confrontation with the King's men.

An account of Crispus Attucks' early life describes him as the son of an African father and an Indian mother. His mother was possibly a descendant of "John Attucks, a converted Christian who was executed for treason in 1676 during King Philip's War, because he sided with his own people, the Natick Indians." In the Natick language the word "Attuck" means "deer."

A monument stands on Boston Common to the memory of Crispus Attucks and his fellow martyrs.

Benjamin Banneker

1731-1806

BANNAKER'S
MARYLAND, PENNSYLVANIA DELAWARE
VIRGINA, KENTUCKY, and NORTH
CAROLINA

Almanack

AND
EPHEMERIS
1796;

POTOMAC

DISTRICT OF COLUMBIA

WASHINGTON
D.C.

VIRGINIA

MARYLAND

Benjamin Banneker

THE MAGNIFICENT grandeur of design that causes the nation's capital to be outstanding among world capitals might have been lost for all time had it not been for the prodigious memory and highly developed mathematical mind of Benjamin Banneker, a black man.

Banneker was born November 9, 1731 in Baltimore County, Maryland, on a one-hundred and fifty acre site known as Bannaky Springs, originally settled by his grandmother, Molly Walsh. One-hundred twenty acres of this land was purchased in the name of Robert Bannaky and his son, Benjamin, for 7 thousand pounds of tobacco in 1736.

Molly Walsh, an Englishwoman, had come to the colonies as an indentured servant. After serving seven years, she settled on the rich farm land, purchased two male slaves to help her clear the land, and married the one called Bannaky. She and her African husband had four children. The eldest, a daughter named Mary, married Robert, also purchased by Molly and freed. Their only son was Benjamin.

Young Benjamin was taught to read, write and count by his grandmother. When he was still a boy he was sent to a "pay" school in the neighborhood, run by Quakers. The school master was insistent about accepting all children.

Benjamin was very mechanically minded, and soon came to the attention of the Ellicott family, whose mills were the major industry in the area. Mr. George Ellicott was attracted to the brilliant but reserved youth, and permitted him the use of his library and some instruments and tools. A chance meeting with a Jewish merchant visiting Baltimore on business, introduced him to watches. He was fascinated.

In 1754, at the age of 24, Banneker constructed a clock, which not only told the time of day, but also struck the hour. This was the first clock made in this country, according to all records. It was certainly the first in Maryland.

Following the surrender of Cornwallis and the end of the Revolutionary War in 1781, a scourge of yellow fever hit the area, leaving several members of the Ellicott family dead. Banneker was given the astronomy books, telescopes and other instruments which had belonged to Andrew Ellicott. George, Jr., the son of the original owner, carried out his uncle's wish that Benjamin Banneker have his books and instruments for "star gazing."

Because trade with England had been greatly affected by the war, and the almanacs which had been imported were in scarce supply, the Ellicotts and others who knew of Benjamin Banneker's accurate predictions of eclipses and weather patterns, based upon the sun, moon and stars, urged him to compile an almanac. He started to work on the almanac for 1792. In 1790, President George Washington appointed Banneker "the surveyor and astronomer" to assist Major Andrew Ellicott, the general geographer, and Major Pierre L'Enfant with the project of surveying and laying out the new Federal City to be located in the new federal district at which the Capitol of the United States would be located.

During the course of the work, Banneker biographer Shirley Graham relates, "Banneker was frequently observed poring over the sheets of the plans which, with his own, hands, L'Enfant was slowly and painstakingly drawing up." In spite of the demands of the commissioners and others who were interested in seeing the plans for purposes of real estate speculation, Major L'Enfant, who had fought in the Revolution under the command of General Lafayette, refused to show his work. Says author Graham, "He continued to work alone, except for conferences with two or three of his surveyors, including Banneker."

In March, 1792, Secretary of State Thomas Jefferson, placed in charge of the project by President Washington, reached the end of his patience with L'Enfant and sent the Commission word that Major L'Enfant had been "notified that his services were at an end." However, before the notification could be accomplished, Major L'Enfant had packed up and gone home to France, taking all of his sketches, drawings and plans with him.

For over a year the plans had been worked on, and not even Jefferson had seen them. L'Enfant's defection from the plan post meant all the work and all of the money would go to waste. Jefferson called a hasty meeting of the Commission to explain their plight. Banneker had arrived at the meeting in Philadelphia accompanied by Major Ellicott. When Jefferson had completed explaining the situation, he asked if any member of the Commission had a suggestion. There was silence, and then, the only black man in the room asked Thomas Jefferson if the plans, as drawn, were satisfactory. Jefferson repeated that he had not seen them, and then asked, "Why?" "Because," said Banneker, "I have the plans in my head." The Commission then directed that "as soon as performable, Benjamin Banneker would deliver to the Secretary of State, the Honorable Thomas Jefferson, a complete set of plans for the city of Washington and the District of Columbia." Because his recollections of L'Enfant's plans were so accurate, the city of Washington was constructed as planned, in spite of the defection of the Frenchman L'Enfant.

Banneker returned to his small cabin on his family land where he had been born, and set about completing the work on his almanac. Goddard and Angell of Baltimore published the first edition of the work titled, *Benjamin Banneker's Pennsylvania, Delaware, Maryland and Virginia Almanac and Ephemeris for the Year of Our Lord 1792*. He had earlier taken the liberty of making a handwritten copy which he sent to Thomas Jefferson, Secretary of State at Philadelphia on August 19, 1791. He sent with the almanac a letter, which said in part:

> Sir, suffer me to call to your mind that time in which the arms and tyranny of the British Crown were exerted with every powerful effort, in order to reduce you to a state of servitude. Look back, I entreat you, to the variety of dangers to which you were exposed; reflect on that time in which every human aid appeared unavailable, and in which even hope and fortitude wore the aspect of inability to the conflict, and you cannot but be led to a serious and grateful sense of your miraculous and providential preservation.
>
> You cannot but acknowledge that the present freedom and tranquility which you enjoy you have mercifully received, and that it is the peculiar blessing of Heaven.
>
> This, sir, was a time in which you clearly saw into the injustice of a state of slavery and in which you had just apprehensions of the horrors of its condition; it was now, sir, that your abhorrence thereof was so excited that you publicly held forth this true and invaluable doctrine, which is worthy to be recorded and remembered in all succeeding ages:
>
> "We hold these truths to be self-evident, that all men are created equal, and that they are endowed by their Creator with certain inalienable rights, that amongst these are life, liberty and the pursuit of happiness."
>
> Here, sir, was a time in which your tender feelings for yours

engaged you thus to declare; you were then impressed with a proper idea of the just valuation of liberty, and the free possession of those blessings to which you were entitled by nature, but sir, how pitiable it is to reflect, that although you were so fully convinced of the benevolence of the Father of Mankind, and of His equal and impartial distribution of those rights and privileges which He had conferred upon them, that you should, at the same time, counteract His mercies, in detaining by fraud and violence so numerous a part of my brethren, under groaning captivity and oppression; that you should, at the same time, be found guilty of that most criminal act, which you professedly detested in others with respect to yourselves...

And now, sir, although my sympathy and affection for my brethren hath caused my enlargement thus far, I ardently hope that your candor and generosity will plead with you in my behalf, when I make known to you that it was not originally my design, but having taken up my pen in order to direct to you, as a present a copy of an almanac which I have calculated for the ensuing year, I was unexpectedly led thereto.

This calculation, sir, is the production of my arduous study in this, my advanced stage of my life; for having long had undoubted desires to become acquainted with the secrets of nature, I have had to gratify my curiosity therein, through my own assiduous application to astronomical study, in which I need not recount to you the many difficulties and disadvantages I have had to encounter.

And though I had almost declined to make my calculations for the ensuing year, in consquence (sic) of the time I had allotted thereto, being taken up at the Federal Territory, by the request of Mr. Andrew Ellicott; yet finding myself under several engagements to printers of this State, to whom I had communicated my design, on my return to my place of residence, I industriously applied myself thereto, which I hope I have accomplished with correctness and accuracy, a copy of which I have taken the liberty to address to you, and which I hope you will favorably receive, and although you may have the opportunity of perusing it after its publication, yet I choose to send it to you in manuscript previous thereto that thereby you might not only have an earlier inspection, but that you might also view it in my own hand-writing.

And now, sir, I shall conclude, and subscribe myself with the most profound respect.

Your most obedient, humble servant,

B. BANNEKER

Jefferson acknowledged receipt of the almanac in a letter to Banneker, in which he acknowledged the degraded position that most blacks were in—both in Africa and America. Later, he sent the manuscript of the almanac to Marquis de Condorcet, the famed French mathematician and advocate of republican political principles.

The almanac was published annually for the next ten years, but the last four years of his life found Banneker too infirm to make the difficult mathematical computations demanded for accuracy, and so it ceased publication.

Benjamin Banneker died on October 28, 1806. He left his instruments, books and records in the care of the Ellicott family, who had first recognized his talent and encouraged its recognition by the outside world.

Prince Hall and Primus Hall

1735(?)-1807   1756-1855

Prince Hall and Primus Hall

PRINCE HALL'S early life is shrouded in mystery and contra-diction. Some accounts give his birth date as 1748, others, 1735. Some historians have him working his way to America on a ship, and within seven years of arrival, by the age of twenty-five, he is minister, property-owner and voter. Other, more recent research documented by the scholars who worked on the *Black Presence in the Era of the American Revolution,* place Prince Hall in Boston in the late 1840's, a slave, owned by William Hall—place of birth, unknown.

Records show that in 1762 he joined the Congregational Church on School Street, and in the spring of 1770, following the Boston Massacre, William Hall gave Prince Hall his freedom.

Early accounts of his birth in the West Indies in Bridgetown on the island of Barbados, have him the son of a leather-worker, and apprenticed to the leather trades before coming to the colonies. It is possible that he came to Boston without papers, was captured and sold into slavery for the period that he was owned by Hall. In any event, a bill of sale sent by Prince Hall to Colonel Crafts of the Boston Regiment of Artillery on April 24, 1777 "for five leather drum heads," shows him actively involved in the leather business.

There is no contradiction in the fact that he was articulate and knowledgeable. He was literate, although his spelling would indicate that he was mainly self-taught.

On March 6, 1775, Prince Hall and 14 other black men were initiated into a British military masonic lodge. When the British soldiers withdrew from Boston, Hall and his fellow Masons formed their own lodge, African Lodge #1, under a limited charter. It may have been that the lodge gave the group an opportunity to meet under a protective organizational cover, that would have been viewed otherwise as conspiratorial.

The outbreak of hostilities between England and the colonies caused Boston's free black population to feel that the inconsistency between slavery and the tenets of the Declaration of Independence were so glaring that these inequities would soon be corrected. Prince Hall and his fellow black Bostonians therefore petitioned for an end of slavery in the Massachusetts colony. Filed in the General Court of Massachusetts on January 13, 1777, the petition read in part:

(The petitioners) cannot but express astonishment that it has never been considered, that every principle from which America has acted, in the course of her unhappy difficulties with Great Britain, bears stronger than a thousand arguments in favor of your humble petitioners. They therefore humbly beseech Your Honors to give their petition its due weight and consideration, and cause an act of the legislature to be passed, whereby they may be restored to the enjoyment of that freedom, which is the natural right of all men, and their children (who were born in the land of liberty) may not be held as slaves after they arrive at the age of twenty-one years. So may the inhabitants of this State (no longer chargeable with the inconsistency of acting themselves the part which they condemn and oppose in others) be prospered in their glorious struggle for liberty, and have those blessings secured to them by Heaven, of which benevolent minds cannot wish to deprive their fellowmen.

Prince Hall also led the protest of free black soldiers who were dismissed from the Continental Army under General Washington's black exclusion policy.

After hostilities had come to an end, the African Lodge that had been formed was chartered by the Grand Lodge of England as the African Lodge #459. In later years Prince Hall was influential in organizing masonic lodges in Philadelphia and Providence, Rhode Island, thus making Prince Hall Masons the first black group to have other than local connotations.

Again making use of the public petition, he also demanded more education for black children, having come to regard education as one of the main sources of power. "We . . . must fear for our rising offspring," he said, "to see them in ignorance in a land of gospel light, when there is provision made for them as well as others and (they) can't enjoy them, and (no other reason) can be given (than that) they are black . . ."

Hall died on November 4, 1807, a fairly wealthy man, known and respected throughout the state of Massachusetts and beyond. His lifelong efforts in behalf of black people had left its mark on history. He is buried in the old Copps Hill Burial Ground in Boston.

The son of Prince Hall, Primus, was, according to United States Archives, born February 29, 1756 on Beacon Street in Boston. At the age of one month, he was given to Ezra Trask, a white farmer, where he remained until his fifteenth year. If the records regarding Prince Hall becoming a free man in the spring of 1770 are accurate, then the probability of him claiming his son, who had until that time been known as Primus Trask, is reasonable. Primus was released from Trask's apprenticeship when he was 15, or in 1771, a year after Prince Hall gained his own freedom.

In January, 1776, now nearly 20 years old, Primus enlisted in the Army. He participated in the retreat from Governor's Island, and the battles of White Plains, Trenton and Princeton. In 1777, he was in Flint's company of Colonel Johnson's Massachusetts Regiment and was also at the capture of General Burgoyne. During the years 1781 and 1782, Primus Hall served 22 months as a servant to Colonel Timothy Pickering, Commissary General of the Army. He was with the Colonel at the siege of Yorktown. He was discharged at Newburgh, New York, December, 1782.

After the war he became engaged in the coal boiler business. He was married to Ann Clark in Boston and allowed a pension by a Special Act of Congress, June 28, 1838. He died in 1855.

Jean-Baptiste Pointe du Sable

1745-1818

Jean-Baptiste Pointe du Sable

ONE OF the most colorful persons in the history of our country was Jean-Baptiste Pointe du Sable. He was a successful fur trader, businessman, and close friend of Pontiac, organizer of the so-called Conspiracy of 1763. It is said that DuSable's half-Indian son was killed fighting against the United States. Today Du Sable is honored as the founder of Chicago.

This adventurous entrepreneur was a Haitian Negro who came to the United States in 1765. An astute businessman, he quickly became a prominent fur trader. Like many Frenchmen during this period, Du Sable was more interested in trapping and trading than in establishing a permanent home, and his life was spent in plying his trade up and down the Mississippi river.

When Spain gained control of New Orleans, Du Sable moved to St. Louis. There he continued his fur trading activities, becoming quite wealthy. When the English took over St. Louis, Du Sable moved again.

He married a Potawotomi Indian and settled among that tribe near the site of present-day Peoria. In 1772, he began a settlement at Eschikagou. Detractors sometimes refer to this settlement as a mere cabin, but in fact it was quite extensive, and included a general store, a mill, and a workshop. Du Sable's trading post also included a forty-foot house, a dairy, and a smokehouse. He brought his wife, his son, and other Potawotomi Indians there. The first recorded birth in Chicago is that of Du Sable's daughter, Suzanne. Both Indians and Frenchmen were employed by Du Sable, one of the earliest successful black businessmen in the United States.

Du Sable's admiration for the French and his cordial relations with the Indians caused the English to regard him with suspicion. During the tense days of the American Revolution he was imprisoned, but was released after a short time.

Jean Baptiste remained at Eschikagou until 1800. In the first year of the new century, he sold all his land in this area to Jean Le Mai. Du Sable moved to Peoria, where he lived until his wife's death. He then moved to St. Charles, which was his home until his death in 1818. Du Sable's grave is at St. Charles Borromeo Cemetery, St. Charles, Missouri.

Du Sable showed great vision in selecting Eschikagou. Its location near the Great Lakes chain, with access to a vital highway of commerce, made it an ideal situation for future development. Chicago's central location enabled it to become what Sol Holt referred to as the hub of our rail system. It is the second largest city in the United States and the tenth largest in the world.

Du Sable's contribution to the growth of the United States is commemorated by a plaque in Chicago which reads: "Site of the first house in Chicago, erected around 1779 [it should be 1772] by Jean Baptiste Pointe Du Sable, a Negro from Haiti." This is hardly a fitting monument to the founder of a city, but lack of recognition does not lessen the importance of the work done by this pioneer. Charlemae Rollins has pointed out that many writers list John Kinzie, the trader to whom Du Sable sold his interests, as the founder of Chicago, but she adds that the earlier bill of sale is in the Wayne County Courthouse, proving that Du Sable was the founder.

Phillis Wheatley

1753-1784

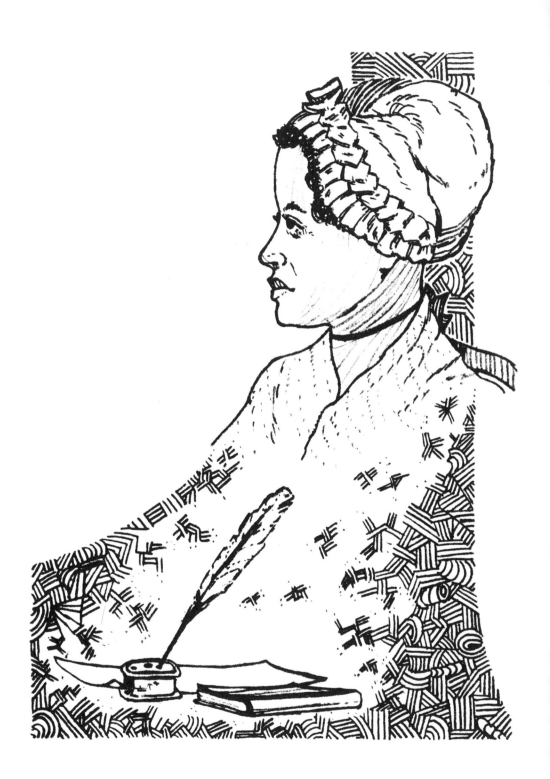

Phillis Wheatley

I T WAS 1761 and at the heart of the New England trade in rum, tobacco, sugar and slaves, was the Port of Boston. Here a small, fragile and very black child was placed on the slave block. Sheltered from the New England weather with only a few rags to cover her naked body, this little girl of seven or eight years was still shedding her front teeth, when she was placed up for sale to the highest bidder and sold like a bundle of hay or a cord of wood to The Honorable John Wheatley, merchant and tailor of Boston, Massachusetts.

The merchant gave the child to his wife, Susannah, whose motherly instincts overcame her natural reticence, and the frail girl was pampered and petted back into a semblance of health, by the woman who came as close to being a mother to the kidnapped African as the circumstances would permit.

In the Wheatley household, where there was a son and daughter, Phillis was taught to read and write, and within a matter of months, her precocious mind had mastered the English language, and she was translating Homer's poetry from the Latin into English. She soon began to write verses of her own, and while still in her early teens, she wrote a poem giving advice and counsel to the students at Harvard College, where the young Wheatley son was a student. Her poetry was modeled after the neo-classical style, a form which at that time was very popular.

The winter of 1772-73 was very hard on Phillis, and her health seemed to go into decline. The son of Mr. and Mrs. Wheatley had to go to London on business, and the family decided that the sea voyage would be beneficial for Phillis, so she was given the opportunity to go to London. While there she came to the attention of the Countess of Huntington and the Earl of Dartmouth. She had written a eulogy to Reverend George Whitfield, who had been under the Countess' patronage, and her English friends were instrumental in having published a slim volume of "Poems on Various Subjects, Religious and Moral," by Phillis Wheatley, Negro Servant to Mr. John Wheatley of Boston, in New England. The poems were thought to be so unusual for a person of Phillis' background and lowly status, that a group of several distinguished men in the colonies were asked to verify the fact that the poetry was indeed written by this young black woman, now just 20 years of age.

Her mistress, Mrs. Wheatley, became ill, and Phillis returned to Boston, where it is believed that Phillis was given her freedom before her mistress' death.

In 1776, the War for Independence severed relations between the colonies and England. Phillis wrote a poem to George Washington which began:

"Celestial Choir! enthron'd in realms of light,
    Columbia's scenes of glorious toils I write.
While freedom's cause her anxious breast alarms,
    She flashes dreadful in refulgent arms.
A crown, a mansion, and a throne that thine,
    With gold unfading, WASHINGTON! be thine."

Her poem so pleased the general that he invited her to visit him at his headquarters, should she ever come to Cambridge, and in a letter to a friend, dated February 10, 1776, Washington indicated his pleasure over the poem.

The war brought financial reverses to Mr. Wheatley, and with his daughter, now married, and his son, still in England, he sold the home that Phillis had known since she had been taken off the slave block as a child. Phillis, a free woman, had no way to earn a living, and her fragile physical condition did not permit her to do the kind of labor that was required of blacks in those days. She married John Peters, a free black man. He earned his living as a grocer, and he preached and practiced some law in behalf of other blacks. He had a reputation for being "uppity" and difficult, and was thrown into debtors prison. Phillis, abandoned and ill herself, could not save her two infant sons. The oldest died first, and then the baby. Hours later, Phillis Wheatley Peters, one of the first women, black or white, to attain literary distinction in America, died. It was on December 5, 1784. Before her death, she had brought together enough poetry for a second volume, which she advertised in a Boston paper. The manuscript was borrowed, and after her death, her husband advertised for its return, but was apparently unsuccessful in retrieving the lost poems.

Phillis Wheatley had survived against tremendous odds, and in November, 1973, 200 years after her poems were first published, a group of black women poets, under the direction of poet-author Margaret Walker Alexander, celebrated her greatness at a Phillis Wheatley Festival at Jackson State College in Jackson, Mississippi. A sculptured bust by Elizabeth Catlett was dedicated to the African child who grew into one of America's first poets.

Paul Cuffe *

1759-1817

*Many sources spell Cuffe with two e's. However, his signature on a document dated 1780 bears only one.

Paul Cuffe

P AUL CUFFE, the son of an African father and an Indian mother, was born in 1759 on Cutterhunker, one of the Elizabeth Islands near New Bedford, Massachusetts.

His father died when he was fourteen, and two years later he went to sea as a deckhand on a ship sailing to the Gulf of Mexico.

During the War of the Colonies against the Crown, his ship was captured by the British and he was held in prison in New York for three months.

In 1780, when he was just over 21 years of age, Paul Cuffe and his brothers decided that blacks should be excused from paying taxes because they were not represented in their own government. They were promptly threatened with jail. Having called the situation to the attention of authorities, the Cuffes paid the tax, and then sent a petition, signed by a number of black men, to the Massachusetts Legislature, asking that their appeal be heard, since they had "no voice or influence in the election of those who tax us." The appeal was granted, and a law was enacted granting free blacks the privileges of all other citizens of Massachusetts, and making them liable to taxation according to the ratio for white men.

With a small amount of capital from the sale of some inherited land and his savings, Cuffe bought a seagoing vessel which he navigated himself. Within a few years he had increased his ownership to several ships and had a partial interest in a number of others. Later he built his own vessels in his own shipyard.

In the 1790's he built a schoolhouse for children and adults in the community. He was a Quaker in his religious views. He had a strong feeling that blacks could only be advanced by returning to Africa. He encouraged the colonization of a community of émigrés at Sierra Leone. In 1815, two years before he died, he saw his dream fulfilled when he personally shepherded 38 black emigrants to Sierra Leone, at his own expense, and furnished them with the necessities of life in the new Afro-American colony. He died September 7, 1817. His ships had traveled to ports as far away as Russia, England, the African coast and the West Indies.

Richard Allen

1760-1831

Richard Allen

BORN A SLAVE in 1760, Richard Allen was converted to Methodism while he was the property of a Delaware farmer. He used his skill as a wood cutter to earn the money with which he purchased his freedom in 1783.

After traveling through the eastern part of the country, he moved to Philadelphia. Occasionally he preached at St. George's Methodist Episcopal Church, where both blacks and whites worshipped. However, discriminatory practices soon ended this integrated worship. In November, 1787, while kneeling in the church, Absalom Jones, another former slave and a close associate of Allen's, was pulled to his feet by a white usher. The usher told him to move to the back of the church. Angered, Jones, Allen, and the other Negroes in the Church walked out.

Led by Allen, the Negroes of Philadelphia organized and built Bethel African Methodist Episcopal Church, which was dedicated in 1794. Later, Allen united the separate churches in several states, and became their first bishop. Thus we see that the black church, like many other black institutions, was formed not because the Negro wanted to be "with his own kind," as segregationists would have us believe, but because he was discriminated against in white or integrated institutions.

Allen played a prominent part in combatting a disastrous yellow fever epidemic which struck Philadelphia in 1793. He and Absalom Jones led the Negroes who assisted Dr. Benjamin Rush, the noted abolitionist, in caring for the sick. Many panic-stricken whites had fled the city, several of the doctors had died, and Rush depended on the blacks to assist him. Although one Philadelphian, Mathew Carey, criticized the Negroes for not doing enough (having himself fled the city and done nothing at all), Allen and the other black Americans received formal thanks from the city officials.

This was not the only time that Richard Allen helped defend Philadelphia. During the War of 1812, after Washington fell to the British, it was feared that Philadelphia would soon be under attack. Richard Allen and Absalom Jones recruited over two thousand Negroes to build fortifications at Gray's Ferry.

Richard Allen also lent his influence to the black Americans' fight against colonization. Disregarding claims that the American Colonization Society (with founders such as pro-slavery advocate John Calhoun) was designed to help the Negro, Allen denounced it as an outrage. Allen's opinion was echoed by later blacks in response to other colonization schemes such as those proposed by President Abraham Lincoln. Allen's statement, made in 1831, declared that this country, having been watered by the tears and blood of the Negro, was now the Negro's country.

Allen was also interested in the condition of the free Negro, as evidenced by his forming the Free African Society, and in the abolition of slavery, as evidenced by his "pray-in" while the Bill of Rights was being written. Richard Allen has a well-earned place in the ranks of those black Americans who tried to make the American dream a reality, not merely a theory.

David Walker

1785-1830

David Walker

D AVID WALKER, one of the most fiery pamphleteers in the history of our country, was born in North Carolina in 1785, the son of a slave father and a free mother. Having no affection for the state which held his father in bondage, Walker moved to Boston. There he began working on *Freedom's Journal*, the Negro newspaper owned by John Russwurm and Samuel Cornish.

Although he was free, Walker's hatred of slavery did not abate. He insisted that supposedly Christian Americans treated the sons of Africa more cruelly than the Egyptians treated the Israelites, for the Israelites had owned land. Further, the Egyptians had never insisted that Israelites were not human.

David Walker's famous *Appeal to the Colored Citizens of the World* was published in 1829. In this pamphlet, he discussed a number of topics. He denounced colonization and urged the Negro to continue fighting for equality, declaring that the Negro was determined to be free and that America belonged to the Negro more than it belonged to the whites. He also warned that future generations would suffer from the effects of slavery because America's riches arose from the blood and tears of the black. Walker commented on Thomas Jefferson's "suspicion" that blacks' mental and physical endowments were inferior, and the "unfortunate difference of colour and perhaps of faculty" hindered emancipation. This, Walker said, was like taking two animals, caging one of them, and then expecting it to run as fast as the free animal. This comment reminds one of Frederick Douglass's statement that whites barred blacks from schools and then accused them of being ignorant.

Walker was also like Douglass (and the great Malcolm Shabazz) in that he criticized those blacks who courted favor with the enemy and aided whites who oppressed the Negro. Walker declared that without unity, blacks would perpetuate their own misery. He was also like Malcolm in criticizing "free" blacks who expressed contentment with their condition. He said that they could not be truly happy until their enslaved brethren all over the world were free.

Slaveowners, always afraid of insurrection and recalling the large-scale rebellions organized by Gabriel Prosser and Denmark Vesey, felt the *Appeal* was dangerous. Circulating the *Appeal* became a capital offense in the South, and a ten-thousand-dollar reward was offered for the capture of David Walker.

Walker's family and friends were afraid his views would lead to his death, and they advised him to flee to Canada. He knew his life was in danger but, like Martin Luther King Jr. in the next century, he felt that he had to take a stand against injustice.

In 1830, after the third edition of the *Appeal* was published, Walker died. Many people suspected that he had been murdered, but it was never proved. David Walker died without achieving his goal, but the popularity of his *Appeal* illustrated Frederick Douglass's belief that if the law did not come to the relief of the Negro, he would devise methods of his own. The results of ignoring both Walker and Douglass can be seen today.

Ira Aldridge

1807-1867

Ira Aldridge

ONE OF the byproducts of racial prejudice is the loss to the United States of the talents of great artists who go to countries where they will be judged, as Martin Luther King Jr. noted (echoing the words of Lott Carey as he sailed for Africa more than one hundred years ago), by their character and merits, not by their complexion.

The life of Ira Aldridge, the great Shakespearean actor, is one of the best (or worst) examples of this facet of discrimination. Freeborn in 1807, Ira attended the African Free School in Manhattan. He was endowed with a striking physique and he developed his dramatic talents by acting in Shakespearean plays at the African Grove Theater. However, the theater was attacked by hoodlums, and after several performances had been broken up by white mobs, it was closed.

Sent to England to complete his education, Aldridge discovered that there his color was no bar to success as an actor. By the time he was twenty, he had achieved fame in his most notable role, that of Othello the Moor. His success was doubly significant, for until that time the part had been played by white actors in black-face. In our own time, despite Paul Robeson's and William Marshall's highly acclaimed portrayals, the film version of *Othello* again starred a white actor in dusky make-up.

53

Of course, Aldridge's great reputation did not rest on his portrayal of one character. He gave distinctive performances as King Lear, Richard the Third, Macbeth, and Shylock in *The Merchant of Venice*. Aldridge departed from Shakespearean roles and used his talents to promote the antislavery cause: he played Gambia in *The Slave* or *The Blessings of Liberty*, a play designed to plead the slave's cause, and a similar role as Mungo the slave in *The Padlock*. His performance in this role was hailed as the most realistic stage portrayal of a Negro character. Mungo's song, "Dear Heart, What a Terrible Life I'm Led" described slavery as a quite different institution from the one pictured by pro-slavery apologists.

Ira Aldridge's career spanned four decades. He displayed his talents throughout Europe, playing leading parts in Stockholm, Berlin, Moscow, Krakow, Vienna and, of course, London. He was honored by royal personages including the King of Sweden and the Czar of Russia. Students in Moscow unhitched the horses from his carriage and pulled it through the streets after his performance to show their admiration for the great Negro actor. Among his close friends was Alexandre Dumas, the noted Negro author of *The Count of Monte Cristo* and *The Three Musketeers*.

The Ira Aldridge Memorial Chair at the Shakespeare Memorial Theatre, Stratford-on-Avon, honors him today. Ironically, his reputation and honors were earned in the Old World, and were denied the great tragedian in the United States, the country of his birth. He died on tour in Poland, in 1867.

James Beckwourth

1798-1867

James Beckwourth

A FASCINATING epoch in our country's history began after Toussaint L'Ouverture's black forces defeated Napoleon's troops in Haiti and helped influence the emperor to sell the Louisiana Territory to the United States. This land, stretching from the Mississippi to the Rockies, opened the way for expansion westward.

Negroes played a significant, though paradoxical role in this drive to the west. They helped to destroy the western Indian tribes while in other areas, notably Florida, blacks and Indians united to fight the white man. Even in the Florida Seminole Wars there was the further paradox of other blacks helping the United States forces against blacks and Indians.

York, a valuable member of the Lewis and Clark expedition who later became a mountain man; Isaiah Dorman, cavalry scout; the buffalo soldiers of the Ninth and Tenth Cavalries noted for their assistance in the capture of Geronimo, and winners of thirteen Medals of Honor are only a few of the many Negroes who "won the West."

An extraordinary figure in this westward movement was Jim Beckwourth, often referred to as "the black Kit Carson." Jim was born in Fredericksburgh, Virginia on April 6, 1798. In 1805 his family moved to twelve miles below St. Charles, on the Missouri River, and from 1808 to 1812 he attended school in nearby St. Louis.

Jim's parents apprenticed him to a blacksmith in St. Louis. He learned his trade, but his pride, his temper, and his fists prevented him from practicing it. One day, the blacksmith made a slighting reference to Jim's Negro ancestry and was surprised when Jim did not accept it with a grin. Jim was only fourteen but he struck the blacksmith, and came off best in the ensuing fight.

Jim left St. Louis and worked as an independent fur trapper and as a hunter for the lead miners in Illinois, during which time he became friendly with the Galena and Sac Indians. Then, in 1823, he joined William Ashley's Rocky Mountain Fur Company and continued his career as one of the mountain men, the legendary fur trappers who roamed the west, blazed trails, and discovered passes.

Beckwourth became familiar with the western territory and knew three Indian dialects, so he often served the government as scout and guerilla fighter. The Indian tribes respected him and, with the name Morning Star, he was adopted by the Crows, who made him their war chief after he had successfully led them in a number of battles against the Blackfeet. Beckwourth married a Crow and his son, Black Panther, became a chief of the tribe.

On April 26, 1850, Beckwourth discovered a pass through the Sierra-Nevada to the Yuba and Truckee rivers. He led the first party of seventeen wagons through Beckwourth Pass (now, on U.S. 40 east of the junction with U.S. 35, a part of the nation's highway system). and later operated a hotel and trading post in Beckwourth Valley.

Beckwourth's exploits aroused a great deal of admiration and curiosity, and in 1854 he was asked to tell his life story. He dictated the events and *The Life and Adventures of James Beckwourth, Mountaineer, Scout, Pioneer and Chief of the Crow Nation of the Indians* was published in 1856. There is undoubtedly exaggeration in his account, but historian Bernard DeVoto called it "the best social history of the west." Although on a different level from such contemporary black leaders as David Walker and Henry Highland Garnet, Beckwourth provides a colorful chapter in our history.

George Bush

1791-1867

CANADA

SEATTLE

WASHINGTON

BUSH
PRAIRIE

PORTLAND   COLUMBIA RIVER

OREGON

LOUISIANA

LAKE
PONTCHARTRAIN

BATTLE OF
NEW ORLEANS
1815 JAN. 8TH

NEW
ORLEANS

George Bush

ETWEEN 1542 and the beginning of the nineteenth century, mariners of Spain, England, and the United States glimpsed the area which was to become the Oregon Territory, but it was not until 1804 that the United States sent the Lewis and Clark expedition to explore this rich expanse of land whose eastern plains and plateaus are separated from the western valleys by the Cascade Mountains. York, Clark's Negro slave, was so valuable to the expedition as interpreter and unofficial goodwill ambassador to the Indians that Clark freed him at the end of the expedition.

Important as York's contribution to this expedition was, it was outweighed by the work of a later Negro, a fur trader and pioneer named George Bush who had already served the United States before he entered the Oregon Territory.

At the Battle of New Orleans, Andrew Jackson, faced with 7,500 British veterans of the Napoleonic wars, called on the free Negroes for help. The black Americans responded to his call and made up one-sixth of Jackson's army. With a total force of 4,500, including Negroes, Choctaw Indians, Lafitte's pirates, and soldiers, Jackson solidly defeated the British. Over 1,500 British were killed or wounded, with American losses only 71. Jackson, in explaining this remarkable victory, said he believed that Pakenham, the British leader, had been killed by "a free man of color."

Jackson had high praise for the black soldiers, telling them that he had expected much, but they had surpassed his expectations. Old Hickory said he was determined to inform the President about the conduct of the Negro fighters, and assured them that the representatives of the American people would applaud their valor.

One of the black fighters who heard these words was George Bush, but he and other Negro Americans would discover that words meant very little. Less than six years after the battle the Army issued an order that neither Negroes nor mulattoes were to be allowed to enter the United States army.

Bush moved northward, lived in Missouri for a time, and went on, in 1820, to Oregon, where he became an employee of the Hudson's Bay Company. He worked for the company until 1830, when he returned to Missouri, married, and became the father of five children.

Bush could not forget the lure of the west, and in 1844 he took his family to Oregon. George led several white settlers, including Michael Simmons, who later related how Bush encountered a new form of discrimination. An Oregon law forbade Negroes from entering the state (as did Indiana's constitution for a time), and prescribed a beating for any Negro who broke this law. Bush's companions vowed to help protect him from such treatment, but the law was not enforced.

Bush's group prospered, and the Bush family gave food and other provisions to later settlers until they could become self-sufficient. Bush built one of the first saw and grist mills in Oregon. Our country's claim to the Oregon Territory was based in part on the settlement established by George Bush, the black man after whom Bush Prairie is named.

Robert Smalls

1839-1915

Robert Smalls

D URING the Civil War, a major asset of the Union Navy was the "Planter," a Confederate gunboat valued at $60,000. This gunboat, used by federal forces throughout the war, played an important part in many sea battles and in the blockade that helped defeat the South.

The man responsible for the Union's acquisition of this valuable vessel was Robert Smalls, a twenty-two-year-old slave born in Beaufort, South Carolina. When he was twelve years old, Robert was taken to Charleston by his master. There he learned to handle a ship. He used this knowledge and ability to escape from the Confederates.

The Confederates had forced Robert and other Negro slaves to serve as deckhands aboard the "Planter." On May 31, 1862, Captain Ripley and his men went ashore at Charleston Harbor, leaving only the slaves aboard the vessel. This was Robert's chance. His wife and children were smuggled aboard, and he put his escape strategy into execution.

It was a dangerous plan. He had to sail past the Confederate guns at Fort Sumter and Morris Island, which stood between him and freedom. He and the other slaves got the vessel under way. When the "Planter" reached the Confederate guards at Fort Sumter. Smalls donned Captain Ripley's straw hat and stood in the pilot

65

house, as the captain always did. The Confederates were deceived, and the "Planter" sailed past the cannons.

After reaching the Union lines, Smalls turned the "Planter" over to federal officials. He had earned both his freedom and a financial reward from the government. A free man, he joined the Navy as a pilot. In this capacity, he participated in the defeat of the Confederate forces at Simmons Bluff. He also took part in the attack on Fort Sumter. When the captain of the "Planter" panicked and deserted his post under fire, Smalls took over and sailed the boat out of danger. After this exploit he was named captain and, on December 1, 1863, assumed command of the "Planter" until 1866, when the vessel was taken out of commission. As captain, he was one of the many Union fighters who enforced the blockade that was so ruinous to the land of King Cotton.

At the end of the war, Smalls sailed the "Planter" into Charleston, with some two thousand Negroes aboard, to witness the raising of the Stars and Stripes over Fort Sumter. This was the symbolic ending of Confederate rule based, as its Vice-President had noted, on the "great truth" that the Negro is inferior and that his natural position is slavery. Unfortunately, this false and pernicious concept of inferiority, originally advanced to justify slavery, did not die with the Confederacy.

After the war, Smalls served as a member of the South Carolina House of Representatives. As a congressman he is remembered for his promotion of a civil rights bill and for his gallant but vain effort to stop the former Confederates from taking away the Negro's hard-won rights, but it is as captain of the "Planter" that Robert Smalls, Civil War fighter, is justly famed.

Robert Brown Elliott

1842-1884

Robert Brown Elliott

THE PERIOD immediately after the Civil War (the beginning of the so-called Tragic Era) is one of the most widely and deliberately misrepresented in the history of our country. Accounts of the Ku Klux Klan gallantly riding forth to save white Southerners from the misrule of carpetbaggers, scalawags, and ignorant former slaves have obscured the truth about the sufferings of the black South at this time when slaveowners withheld emancipation by force; the Confederates returned to power in 1865 determined to keep the South a white man's country; the Black Codes established a new form of servitude by restricting the movements of freed slaves; and mob violence in New Orleans and Memphis in 1866 left more than eighty Negroes dead and over one hundred injured.

Elliott was born in 1842 in Boston, Massachusetts, of West Indian parents, and attended schools in Boston, Jamaica, and Eton College in England. On his return to his native land he moved to Columbia, South Carolina and acquired a reputation as a linguist, scholar, lawyer, and the owner of one of the largest private libraries in the state.

After his admission to the bar, Elliott practiced law and edited the *Missionary Record*. He served on the South Carolina Constitutional Convention, was elected state representative in 1868, appointed assistant state adjutant general in 1869, and in 1871 was elected to Congress. In Washington, he vainly urged the passage of a bill to enforce the Fourteenth Amendment, and sought to be appointed to succeed Hiram Revels as senator. Failing in this, Elliott resigned and returned to South Carolina.

He was reelected and returned to Washington. In January, 1874, Charles Sumner's civil rights bill was opposed by former Confederate congressmen. The vituperative attack was led by Alexander Stephens, former Vice-President of the Confederacy, who had not changed his opinions about black inferiority. Elliott's reply to Stephens in support of Sumner's bill, designed to end discrimination in schools, transportation facilities, and theaters, is considered one of the most eloquent ever made in Congress. He described briefly the contributions of the Negro in the Revolutionary War (5,000 enlisted once Washington removed the ban), the War of 1812 (at Lake Erie and New Orleans), and the Civil War (38,000 died fighting for the Union).

Negroes had earned their rights, Elliott said, and pointed out the irony of Stephens, a rebel, trying to block the rights of those who had fought for their country. Negroes had aided the Union when Stephens was trying to "blot the American republic from the galaxy of nations." Elliott's speech was praised by such great orators as Frederick Douglass and Wendell Phillips, and was partly responsible for the passage of the Civil Rights Bill, which, unfortunately, did not bring the Negro the help its author Sumner had intended. Elliott was unhappily prophetic when he said that the qualities of devotion and loyalty displayed by black Americans were qualities that did not always receive their just rewards.

Robert Elliott resigned from Congress in 1875 and returned to South Carolina, where he failed in an effort to be elected Senator, and also in a campaign for governor, defeated by the white-controlled state machinery. He died in virtual obscurity in New Orleans, where he had been practicing law, at the age of forty-two.

Frederick Douglass

1819-1895

Frederick Douglass

PAUL LAURENCE DUNBAR hailed him as Ethiopia's noblest born and the champion of the Negro. Lerone Bennett praised him as the father of the protest movement. Frederick Douglass was a slave who acquired an education, escaped to freedom, and gained renown as an abolitionist, spokesman for the "free" Negro, and fighter for human rights and world peace.

Born in Maryland in 1817, Frederick took his owner's name, Bailey. As a child, Fred suffered hunger and separation from his mother, and saw cruel treatment and even the killing of slaves, go unpunished. As a teenager, he became so restive in the "security" of slavery that his master sent him to Edward Covey, a slavebreaker, whose job was to turn him into a "good" slave. But Fred could not be tamed. After being whipped several times, he decided that "he who is whipped oftenest is he who is whipped easiest." He resisted Covey, and defeated him, and was never beaten again.

At the age of twenty-one Fred escaped, borrowing a sailor suit and free papers. His eloquence in describing the horrors of slavery led to his joining William Lloyd Garrison, a militant white abolitionist. When it was charged that he was a college-educated free Negro, not a self-taught former slave, Fred felt his influence as an abolitionist was diminished. He therefore wrote and published his autobiography, using his real name.

73

To escape re-enslavement, Douglass went to England. Friends there purchased his freedom, and he returned to the United States, where he founded his own paper, the *North Star*. In it he struck against slavery and against Northern discrimination toward the nominally free Negro. He urged unity, and said that helping one another was the way to succeed.

Douglass also worked on the Underground Railroad. After helping three black men escape to Canada, he was arrested, but was successfully defended by Thaddeus Stevens, a white champion of the Negro.

When the Civil War began, Douglass tried to persuade President Lincoln to accept black enlisted men, and to make the war an anti-slavery crusade. Lincoln's refusals, his use of Union troops to return escaped slaves to their owners, and his nullification of emancipation orders by Generals Fremont and Hunter, caused Douglass to criticize him as a tool of the Confederates. When blacks were permitted to enlist, Douglass helped in their drive for equal pay.

After the war, Douglass sought to better the condition of the freedmen. He denounced emancipation as a fraud and declared that the black man was in theory a free man but in fact a slave. The slaves had been sent away without land, food, clothing, or education, and were being legislated back into slavery by the Confederates, now in control. Frederick appealed to President Andrew Johnson for assistance, but Johnson refused to intervene in the southern states. Douglass also helped to promote Sumner's Civil Rights Bill.

Douglass's fight against discrimination was personal as well as public. His daughter was refused admittance to the neighborhood school because she was black and Douglass, with his friends, agitated and petitioned for her admission. He was successful in fighting the color bar, and his daughter attended the school.

What was probably the first "eat-in" was staged by Frederick Douglass. Told to leave a dining room because other diners objected to his being served, Douglass took the direct approach. He stood, glared majestically around the room, and asked if anyone objected to his eating there. No one was heard to object, so Douglass ate in peace.

Active in political circles, Douglass urged the Negro to agitate continually for equality, "If there is no struggle," he said, "there is no progress." However, his encouragement was given not only to the black man but to all oppressed people. He wrote that he did not base any man's rights on his color. Like orator Robert Ingersoll, he did not believe in superiority based on the "accidents of race or color."

Douglass maintained his militant attitude until his death in 1895, fighting many practices (such as discrimination in employment) which are still barriers to equality. His eloquence, fearlessness, and devotion to the true principles of democracy make him one of history's most inspiring figures.

Blanche K. Bruce

1841-1898

U.S.
Senator
From
The State of
Mississippi

1875

Blanche K. Bruce

THE UNITED STATES SENATE, on February 15, 1879, witnessed a unique event. Blanche K. Bruce, a former slave and an astute politician who once received six votes as a vice-presidential nominee, was presiding over a meeting of that legislative body.

Blanche was born in Prince Edward County, Virginia, on March 1, 1841, to a Negro slave mother and a white slaveowner. Men such as Blanche's father could choose how they treated their mulatto offspring. They could ignore the fact of their paternity and treat them exactly as the other slave children. They could send them out of slavery, as did the fathers of Robert Purvis, abolitionist, Norbert Rillieux, inventor, and James Rapier, congressman. Or they could give their children "privileged" positions.

Blanche's father chose the third course. He made Bruce body-servant to his own half-brother. When this legitimate son went away to school, Bruce attended him and obtained some incidental education. When the Civil War began, Bruce's half-brother ran away to join the Confederate army, but Bruce went to Union territory in Hannibal, Missouri, where he became a teacher. In 1866, he went to Oberlin College, Ohio, the first school to admit Negroes and women.

Blanche became a teacher in Floreyville, Mississippi and later held a variety of offices, including superintendent of schools, sheriff, and sergeant-at-arms in the state senate. He began a campaign for election as senator from Mississippi, which ended successfully in 1874.

On March 5, 1875, Blanche began his career as United States senator. At the swearing-in ceremony, according to custom, the senior senator from the state escorts the new senator to the rostrum, but when Bruce's name was called, Senator Alcorn did not rise. Senator Bruce started up the aisle alone, but Roscoe Conkling of New York, embarrassed by such mistreatment of a fellow senator, got to his feet and provided escort.

As a senator, Bruce was described as "able and honest" at a time when corruption in government was widespread. Like Lewis Douglass and Kelly Miller who protested against colonialism in 1898, he was interested in fair treatment for everybody, without regard to color.

He tried to protect the interests of the Indian tribes and in a Senate debate on April 7, 1880, he condemned the United States' Indian policy as selfish, saying that the treaties by which valuable Indian territories were acquired were changed whenever the "irrepressible" white race wanted more room. He saw that aggressions on the territory of these "first Americans" would lead to the Indians' extinction, and urged a new policy to save them. Blanche also opposed the embargo on Chinese immigration. As a representative of a race that had also been considered unfit for American citizenship, he could not support a bill to exclude the Chinese.

Senator Bruce introduced several bills to better the condition of the free Negro, and tried unsuccessfully to help his fellow congressman P. B. S. Pinchback to claim his Senate seat. On March 31, 1876, Bruce made a speech which included these still pertinent comments: (1) peace and order can come only through the recognition of the rights of all people; (2) new laws are not necessary if those that already existed are enforced; (3) Negroes act as a unit because whites have established a color line.

Blanche K. Bruce died on March 17, 1898. His life exemplified Negro determination to overcome all obstacles in striving for equality.

80

Jan Matzeliger

1852-1889

Jan Matzeliger

R ACIAL DISCRIMINATION has made it difficult to assess the Negro's contributions as inventor. Before 1863, patents were not issued to Negro slaves, who therefore received no credit for their inventions. Many devices conceived by slaves were credited to white inventors. It is believed that later inventors concealed their race because of discriminatory practices. For example, after Garrett Morgan used his gas inhalator to help rescue two dozen men whom an explosion had trapped two hundred feet below Lake Erie, he began to receive orders for the inhalator. As soon as it became known that he was a Negro, the orders stopped.

Despite discrimination, Negroes contributed to the economic growth of their country, and the names of some of them are known. One of the most influential inventors was Jan Ernst Matzeliger. Born in Dutch Guiana in 1852, Jan came to the United States in 1876. He settled in Massachusetts and secured work as a cobbler's apprentice.

At this time, a great deal of time and money was being spent in attempts to develop a "lasting" machine—one that could make a complete shoe. These efforts failed. None of the would-be inventors could design a machine that would shape the upper leather over the last and then attach the leather to the bottom of the shoe. This final step had to be done by hand. Since a shoemaker could complete

83

only about fifty pairs of shoes a day, mass production was impossible.

Matzeliger, who had worked in factories since he was ten, determined to invent a lasting machine. People laughed at him when his efforts were discovered, but he continued to work on his project. After perfecting a machine which would adjust the shoe, arrange the leather over the sole, and drive in the nails, Matzeliger applied for a patent. This was not an easy matter: the plans drawn by the thirty-year-old Negro were so complex that the patent office experts could not understand them. The office sent a man to Lynn, Massachusetts, and Matzeliger explained the operation of his machine.

United States patent number 274,207 was granted to Matzeliger in 1883. He sold the patent to Sydney Winston of the United Shoe Machinery Company, and his invention transformed the entire shoe industry. It made Lynn, the home of the company, the shoe capital of the world. In New England, the income from shoe manufacturing rose more than 300 percent. Matzeliger's influence spread beyond the United States as country after country adopted his lasting method.

Jan Matzeliger lived less than forty years, but this one great accomplishment entitles him to be counted with Norbert Rillieux, Garrett Morgan, Elijah McCoy, Granville T. Woods, and James A. Parsons as a significant American Negro inventor.

Granville T. Woods

1856-1910

Inventor
Automatic air brake
Induction telegraph
The third rail

Granville T. Woods

MOST TEXTBOOKS limit their discussion of Negro inventors or scientists to a description of the work of George Washington Carver, and we are largely unaware of the debt which the United States—and other nations—owes to Negro inventors. Whenever we stop at an automatic traffic signal, don a pair of machine-made shoes, or sweeten our food with refined white sugar, we are acknowledging the work of Negro inventors Garrett Morgan, Jan Matzeliger, and Norbert Rillieux.

One of these black inventors had a tremendous impact on the industrialization of the United States. This man, Granville T. Woods, was born in Columbus, Ohio, on April 23, 1856. An admittedly partial Cincinnati newspaper (Woods lived in Cincinnati at the time) hailed him as the equal, if not the superior of any inventor in the country.

Like many other inventors, Woods had little formal education. He stopped attending school when he was ten years old, but he continued to learn and to apply his knowledge throughout the rest of his life. Having left school, Granville obtained work in a machine shop, where he became proficient as a machinist and as a blacksmith. After working in rolling mills and as fireman and engineer on the Iron Mountain Railroads, he decided that he needed further education. He therefore enrolled in an eastern college where he studied mechanical engineering, and went on to work as engineer for two years on a British ocean steamer, the "Ironsides."

In none of these jobs, however, was Granville Woods able to advance. Finding that promotions were not available to him, he struck out on his own. Around 1884 he formed the Woods Railway Telegraph Company in Cincinnati and embarked on a career as an inventor which led to the Cincinnati newspaper's description of him as "the world's greatest electrician."

One of his most famous devices was the air brake which he developed in 1902. This patent was purchased by the Westinghouse Air Brake Company. Another invention was the induction telegraph, which allowed people on moving trains to both send and receive communications and proved to be of immense importance to the railroads in averting collisions.

In 1890, the prolific Negro genius developed "the third rail," which permitted the electrification of New York City's vast transportation system—and caused a riot among the locomotive engineers (all white) whom it displaced. Woods also received a patent for an early phonograph.

The Bell Telephone Company, the American Engineering Company, and the General Electric Company, as well as Westinghouse, purchased patents on his inventions. Within less than thirty years, Woods was granted more than one hundred and fifty patents. He has earned his place in history.

Ida B. Wells Barnett

1869-1931

Ida B. Wells Barnett

T HE END of the nineteenth century has been called one of the lowest points of the Negro's existence in the United States. The Supreme Court had emasculated Charles Sumner's 1875 Civil Rights Act and had approved "separate but equal" facilities. Southern states were expanding Jim Crow laws and disfranchising Negroes. Anti-Negro activities included a large number of lynchings (about two every week for several years), and newspaper articles which hopefully predicted that the Negro race would eventually disappear.

One of the most striking women in our history, Ida B. Wells, came to the fore at that time. A Memphis teacher who became a leader of the antilynching crusade, she reported the shocking truths about lynching in her newspaper, *Free Speech*. Her life was threatened, and she wore a brace of pistols for protection, but the pistols proved insufficient.

In 1892, when she was twenty-three years old, Ida B. Wells wrote about the lynching of three Memphis Negroes. Her article named the lynchers, pointing out that the motive was fear of competition from the Negroes, who were businessmen. After this exposé, her office was destroyed and she was unable to return to the city.

After a lecture tour in the United States and England, Ida Wells married Ferdinand Barnett, an opponent of Booker T. Washington's conciliatory policies, and continued her work. As Chairman of the Anti-Lynching bureau of the Afro-American Council, she related statistics which proved Frederick Douglass's contention that protecting the virtue of white Southern women was not the motivation for lynching. In 1895 she published *A Red Record: Tabulated Statistics and Alleged Causes of Lynchings in the United States, 1892-1893-1894*. The pamphlet was "Respectfully submitted to 19th Century Civilization in the Land of the Free and the Home of the Brave." It included details of lynchings and other information which underscored the irony of this phrase. This pioneering effort in the field of statistics on lynchings was a forerunner of similar work done at the Tuskegee Institute and by the NAACP.

In 1898, Mrs. Barnett headed a group that protested to President McKinley about lynchings. The group declared that if the United States could protect Americans in foreign countries, it could defend citizens at home. This plea for justice proved as futile as had Douglass's earlier demands to Presidents Johnson and Harrison.

Ida also worked with W. E. B. Du Bois against Booker T. Washington's policy of accommodation. Citing mob violence against black people, she declared that Washington was wrong in saying that the Negro could achieve his rights through economic power. She worked again with Du Bois in founding the National Association for the Advancement of Colored People. After the Springfield, Illinois, riot of 1908, Oswald Garrison Villard (William Lloyd Garrison's grandson) asked concerned Negroes and whites to meet to discuss the racial crisis. Booker T. Washington refused to attend, but at a second conference, despite his opposition, the NAACP organization took form.

Mrs. Barnett continued her crusading activities for another twenty-two years, working until her death in 1931. Her forty-year fight for fair treatment for the Negro earned her a prominent place in the ranks of American leaders.

Matthew Henson

1866-1955

Matthew Henson

ADMIRAL RICHARD PEARY is honored as the first man to reach the North Pole, but this honor must be shared with a Negro, Matthew Henson. Henson and Peary met in 1887, when they worked for seven months surveying a proposed canal site in Nicaragua. Henson accompanied Peary on his exploration of Greenland in 1891, although the latter had some doubts about Henson's ability to adapt to the northern climate. During the next seventeen years, he was to see that Henson adapted quite well.

On this first trip north, Henson met Eskimos. They accepted him because of his color, and gave him the name Miy Paluk, My Brother. They also taught him their language and helped him to become the most proficient of Peary's men in the handling of teams of eight or twelve dogs. After establishing that the land mass was an island, the expedition ended.

A second attempt, in 1893, failed, and only Henson and Hugh Lee, a reporter, remained with Peary in Greenland when the expedition returned to New York. On the third expedition, which began in April, 1895, the food supply became dangerously low and they had to hunt musk ox. They had killed three when a wounded cow charged Peary, who was out of ammunition. Only the quick and accurate shooting of Henson saved Peary's life.

Peary and Henson made four more unsuccessful attempts to

reach the Pole—in 1890, 1900, 1901, and 1905. In 1908, Peary began what he felt would be his last attempt. Again, except for Henson, Peary had only college-educated men in his expedition. Again, Henson proved his value. After they reached Camp Sheridan, it was Henson who built the sledges, showed the newcomers how to build an igloo, and taught them what they must know in order to survive the four-hundred-mile trek to the Pole.

However, none of Peary's college men reached the Pole. Henson, Peary, and four Eskimos named Egingwah, Ookeah, Ootah, and Seegloo reached the Pole on April 4, 1909, and it was Matthew Henson, a Negro, who planted the Stars and Stripes.

Henson received little recognition, although members of the expedition praised his effectiveness. In fact, Peary was criticized for including Henson, who had no scientific background, in the expedition despite the fact that without Henson and the Eskimos, Peary would not have reached the Pole. Because expedition team members continually agitated in his behalf, Henson's contribution was belatedly recognized. He received the Navy Medal and was saluted by Presidents Truman and Eisenhower. More appropriate recognition is given him by the Eskimos, among whom Miy Paluk has become a legend. Ahdoolo, the word he used to summon them from their igloos, has become a part of their language.

Daniel Hale Williams

1858-1931

first successful
surgical closing
of a heart wound
1893

PROVIDENT HOSPITAL
CHICAGO - founded in 1891

Daniel Hale Williams

IN 1905 W. E. B. DU BOIS wrote a letter encouraging a young black schoolgirl to stay in school. For a Negro to neglect education was criminal, he said, as the hopes of millions were to some degree dependent on her efforts. If she trained herself, she could be useful as a teacher, homemaker, clerk, stenographer, physician, or nurse.

Twenty years earlier, Du Bois would have been unable to recommend a nursing career for there were no schools for black nurses. Dr. Daniel Hale Williams helped to end this situation.

Born in 1858, his father died when he was twelve and his mother left him to fend for himself. On his way west, Dan passed through Cincinnati and went on to Wisconsin, where he worked as a barber, finished school, and served for two years as apprentice to Dr. Henry Palmer. He then attended Chicago Medical College and was graduated from Northwestern University in 1883. Dr. Williams taught anatomy at Northwestern, served on the Illinois Board of Health, and began his medical practice in Chicago. His coloring (or lack of it) would have allowed him to pass as white, but his pride in his Negro heritage would not. He lived in the ghetto, and was aware of the needs of the black community, especially the need for a hospital where blacks could benefit from the services of properly trained staff; and for a nurses' training school open to Negroes.

Williams therefore began an arduous but successful campaign.

In 1891, interracially financed and interracially staffed Provident Hospital, with the first American training school for black nurses, was organized under his leadership. The hospital provided desperately needed services, but unexpected problems developed: many of the darker Negroes resented Dr. Williams "whiteness." Others, with insufficient education, disliked the high standards Williams had set, which they could not meet. Williams's refusal to lower his standards, and his many contacts in the white world earned him the undying hatred of Dr. George Hall, a graduate of one of Chicago's eclectic schools and therefore unable to meet those standards. Hall eventually succeeded in turning part of the black community against him, which must have marred his pleasure in his most famous achievement.

In 1893 James Cornish was wounded in a street fight: a knife had penetrated the chest wall. Without blood transfusions, X-rays, or sulfa drugs, operations on such injuries had always been fatal. Nevertheless, Dr. Williams performed a heart suture. Four weeks later, James Cornish left the hospital and Daniel Hale Williams became the first surgeon to have operated successfully on the human heart.

From 1893 through 1898, Dr. Williams served as head of Freedmen's Hospital in Washington, D.C. In addition to his work as a surgeon there, he organized a second nurses' training school before he resigned and, at various times, practiced medicine in Chicago, taught clinical surgery at Meharry, served as attending surgeon at the Cook County Hospital, and as staff associate at St. Luke's Hospital, both in Chicago.

Daniel Hale Williams was named a fellow of the American College of Surgeons for his many contributions to medicine, but probably his most fitting monument is Provident Hospital, which he established to better the condition of his fellow man.

Charles Drew

1904-1950

Charles Drew

C HARLES DREW was born June 3, 1904, in Washington, D.C. In high school his excellence in athletics won him a scholarship to Amherst, where he was chosen most valuable baseball player, was captain of the track team, winner of the national AAU high hurdle competition, and was nominated for the All-American Eastern team. He also received the Mossman Trophy for having contributed most significantly to Amherst athletics.

Drew planned to enter medical school after graduation in 1926, but he had to defer this for two years while he took a coaching job at Morgan State College and saved money. In 1928 he applied for admission to Howard University, but was rejected because his English credits from Amherst were inadequate. He applied to several other schools and chose McGill University in Montreal from those that accepted him. His athletic prowess had not exempted him from discrimination and he had heard that, in Canada, equality was real.

At McGill, he combined athletic excellence (he was chosen captain of the track team and established several records) with scholarship (he was one of the top five graduates) and became interested in the problems of blood preservation. He received his M.D. in 1933 and, after an internship at Montreal General Hospital, Drew became an instructor in pathology at Howard in 1935. He decided to continue his research into blood preservation, a vital problem for, although

103

blood banks had been established, patients still died when there was a scarcity of their blood type. Drew received a fellowship at Columbia University to work with Dr. John Scudder, and finally devised a method of preserving blood through refrigeration. In August, 1939, he established an experimental blood bank in New York City which became permanent after a four-month trial. In 1940, the Blood Transfusion Association asked Scudder and Drew to help establish blood banks in France, and the two men became part of the Plasma for France project.

After Dunkirk, the Blood Transfusion Association, using Drew's techniques, tried to supply Britain's needs. Much of the plasma arrived unfit for use. Drew, who had returned to Howard, obtained a leave of absence and returned to New York in October, 1940, as medical director of the plasma project, to investigate these problems. He developed a number of techniques and in February, 1941, became director of the American Red Cross blood banks, establishing stations to collect plasma for the American forces. Later, although black soldiers were fighting and dying for the United States, and a black doctor had devised the blood bank program that saved innumerable lives, Negroes were not allowed to give blood. Dr. Drew and others protested, and finally so-called Negro blood was accepted, but was segregated so that only blacks would receive it.

Drew, who had insisted that segregation of blood was indefensible, resigned and returned to Howard University, where he received the Spingarn Medal and persuaded Congress to increase the inadequate budget of Freedman's Hospital to $3,500,000.

As a teacher, Charles Drew sought to inspire younger blacks to achieve, but he had only seven years to continue his work. He died in the same way as Bessie Smith, the great blues singer. Injured in an automobile accident in the South, he was refused admittance at a white hospital. He bled to death on the way to a black hospital.

Mary McLeod Bethune

1875-1955

Mary McLeod Bethune

MARY McLEOD BETHUNE is often compared to Frederick Douglass for, like him, she overcame tremendous obstacles to rise to prominence. While Douglass, the former slave, became an internationally famous author, speaker, and fighter for human rights, Mary McLeod, once a field hand, became a college president and Spingarn Medal winner.

Born in 1875, Mary was the seventeenth child of former slaves who had become sharecroppers in South Carolina. The school year was only three months long, so education was hard to come by, but Mary walked the five miles to the school and devoted many hours to study. Her diligence was rewarded when she was given money to attend school—the gift of Mary Chrisman, a white seamstress from Colorado who wanted her money used to educate a Negro girl.

Mary attended Scotia Seminary in North Carolina, and after her graduation continued her education at Moody Bible Institute in Illinois, where she decided she would like to become a teacher instead of a missionary, her original goal. She taught at different schools, including Haines Institute in Georgia; Sumter, South Carolina (where she married Alfred Bethune and bore a son), and Palatka, Florida.

In 1904, Mary heard the announcement that railroads were to be built in eastern Florida. She knew that the children of the Negro laborers would have no schools, so she went to Florida and, with one dollar and fifty cents, began her school on an old dumping ground. With her first pupils, five girls, she cleared away the debris. She traveled by bicycle to solicit funds from churches, clubs, and individuals. Slowly the school grew. Faith Hall was built in 1907; eleven years later an auditorium was added. By 1923, less than twenty years after the first five-pupil school was opened, there were six hundred students and over thirty teachers. In that year Bethune merged with Cookman Institute, forming the Bethune-Cookman College.

Mary McLeod Bethune worked for her fellow Americans in many other ways. She lent her support to the NAACP in 1909 and served as president of the National Association of Colored Women's Clubs. During the depression, she left her position as college president to become Director of the Division of Negro Affairs of the National Youth Administration and, through her leadership, enabled over sixty thousand Negroes to remain in school. As NYA Director, Mrs. Bethune was part of the able Black Cabinet which included Robert Weaver and Frank Horne of the Housing Authority, William Houston of the Justice Department, and William Hastie and Eugene Kinckle Jones of the Commerce Department.

Mrs. Bethune also participated in anti-discrimination protests. When Executive Order 8802 (issued by President Roosevelt after A. Philip Randolph's threat of a mass march on Washington) was not enforced and the power of the Fair Employment Practices Commission was weakened, Mrs. Bethune was one of many Negroes who spoke at a Madison Square Garden protest rally in 1942. At the age of seventy, she served as advisor to President Truman, and was an observer at the initial meeting of the United Nations in San Francisco. Her philosophy was epitomized in a phrase she often used in lecturing black audiences: *"This* is our day!"

Charles Clinton Spaulding

1874-1952

Charles Clinton Spaulding

ONE OF the most pervasive forms of racial prejudice suffered by Negroes has been (and still is) discrimination in business and employment opportunities. This discrimination began generations ago. During the colonial period, a Frenchman visiting New England wrote that Negroes who owned businesses were never able to expand beyond a certain limit because whites would not give them financial credit.

When Negroes sought employment, they faced many forms of discrimination. In some parts of the country, it was a crime to teach a Negro a trade. Despite the pleas of Isaac Meyers, an early black labor leader, Negro workers were kept out of the labor union movement. Often, whites would threaten to quit if a black were hired to work with them; often the only job available to the trained Negro was that of a common laborer.

Such discrimination made it impossible for black people to share equally in the riches of their native land. However, just as individuals triumphed over other forms of prejudice, so some Negroes achieved business prosperity. One of the best examples of the successful Negro businessman is Charles Clinton Spaulding.

Charles was born in 1874 in Columbus County, North Carolina. One of fourteen children born to former slaves, he could not obtain an education in his home town, and attended grade school in Durham, working as a bellboy and dishwasher at night and going to school during the day. He finished the eighth grade in 1897, when he was twenty-three years old.

In 1898 he left his job as manager in a store to work for his uncle, John Merrick. Merrick and Moore, prosperous businessmen, were in the process of converting a burial aid association into the North Carolina Mutual Life Insurance Company. At first, the company was so small that Charles was its only employee, serving as janitor, agent, and manager. Although he was not one of the founders, he is often referred to as the company's organizer because of his work in building it up through advertising campaigns and extensive personal contacts.

Spaulding became president of the North Carolina Mutual Life Insurance Company in 1923. He held this position until his death in 1952. Under his leadership, the company grew from one grossing thirty dollars in its first year to the world's largest all-Negro enterprise.

Charles Spaulding's story is not typical, but it illustrates the Negro's business potential—potential which can only be fully developed when discriminatory practices are ended.

W. E. B. Du Bois

1868-1963

W. E. B. Du Bois

THE PROBLEM of the twentieth century is the problem of the color line—the relation of the darker to the lighter races of men in Asia and Africa, in America and the islands of the sea. This statement, which might have been written by a modern "third-world" advocate, was written over sixty years ago by William Edward Burghardt Du Bois, a pioneer in black history, a human rights leader, a sociologist who attacked racist theories, a teacher, author, and leader in the Pan African movement.

Du Bois was born on February 23, 1868, in Great Barrington, Massachusetts. At the suggestion of Frank Rosmer, his high school principal, he took college preparatory courses. He couldn't afford to go to Harvard as he had planned, but was awarded a scholarship to Fisk University. During his three years there, he learned about discrimination, violence, the race problem at its lowest terms, and the "gorgeous color gamut" of the black American. A scholarship to Harvard came after he was graduated from Fisk, in 1888. There he studied with philosopher-psychologist William James, historian Alfred Hart, and philosopher George Santayana. After earning his M.A., he wanted to study in Europe and received a fellowship from 1892 to 1894 to study in Berlin. He traveled in Germany and Italy, and visited Vienna, Budapest, and Krakau.

Returning to the United States in 1894, he began a sixteen-year

115

"academic" period which took him successively to Wilberforce, the University of Pennsylvania, and Atlanta University. At Wilberforce he met Charles Young and Paul Laurence Dunbar, and taught English and foreign languages. Feeling restricted by tradition, in 1896 he accepted an appointment as assistant instructor at the University of Pennsylvania. There he was asked to conduct a study based on the theory that slum-dwelling blacks were the cause of the city's problems. The results were published in *The Philadelphia Negro,* a book which has become a classic and showed that the condition of black people in the cities was a symptom, not a cause of urban problems.

In 1897, Du Bois went to Atlanta University to direct their annual conference on the problems of the black man. For thirteen years, he published annual studies dealing with black business, education, urbanization, and other issues. These studies are still highly regarded and widely used, but Du Bois began to feel that academic studies were not enough at a time when lynchings were frequent and flagrant. His continuing dispute with Booker T. Washington, a Negro leader who believed in a policy of separatism and a "temporary" acceptance of a position inferior to white men, was also a matter of some concern to Atlanta University, whose philanthropic support was endangered by a militant attitude.

Du Bois often expressed admiration for Washington and was in agreement with him on some issues. His criticism was of Washington's acceptance of a subservient role for black people and his encouragement of a policy of giving up political power, civil rights, and higher education as immediate aims. This policy, Du Bois thought, fostered the impression that (1) the South's attitude to black people was justified by their degraded condition; (2) the Negro's failure to rise was due to faulty education, and (3) the Negro must lift himself. Du Bois believed that (1) the Negro's position was the result of slavery and prejudice; (2) it was up to the entire nation to atone for the wrongs done to the Negro; (3) reconciliation must not be purchased

116

by giving up rights; and (4) Negroes must continually fight for their rights. These criticisms appeared in a book of essays entitled *The Souls of Black Folk*. As Saunders Redding wrote, publication of this book fixed the moment when the black American began to think of himself and other blacks as a potential force for organizing society. It did much to crystallize anti-Washington feeling.

At Du Bois's urging, a meeting of black American leaders was called at Niagara to organize the struggle for achievement of full citizenship rights. Later, many members of this Niagara movement were influential in organizing the National Association for the Advancement of Colored People. Du Bois, as editor of the NAACP's magazine, *Crisis*, urged Negroes to prepare for a long struggle and, if necessary, to meet death like men, not like "bales of hay."

When the nation entered World War I, some black Americans asked why they should fight abroad when conditions at home were undemocratic (President Wilson had segregated civil service employees in Washington by executive order; segregation in housing was increasing, and 67 lynchings occurred in 1915). In a *Crisis* editorial entitled "Close Ranks" Du Bois urged Negroes to support the war as they had a better chance in a country which at least preached democracy than they would have in an autocracy.

When the soldiers came home from the war, they found that conditions had not improved. There were eighty-three lynchings in 1919, and eight of the victims were still in uniform. Du Bois wrote, "We saved democracy in Europe and we'll save it in the United States or know the reason why."

Du Bois continued to work for civil rights and also to promote Pan-Africanism. In 1919, with Blaise Diagne, he called a Pan-African Congress in Paris. The delegates sent a petition to the peace conference at Versailles, asking vainly that an international code be adopted that would guarantee the rights of native Africans and provide for self-government. Primarily because of Du Bois's influence, the delegates also asked that Africa's pre-conquest tradition be recognized. Two years later the Second Congress asked the League of Nations to study the problems of blacks, condemn color bars, and appoint a black representative on the Mandate Commission. The response to these representations was to describe the delegates as being in the pay of Russia.

Du Bois's Third Congress, in 1923, demanded an African labor code, free education, trial by jury, and the right to vote. The only positive response to this was the enfranchisement of a few West Africans. The Fourth Pan-African Congress, in 1927, dealt mainly with religious and social betterment, and the proposed Fifth Congress was postponed because of the depression and was finally held in London, in 1945, where Du Bois's audience included Samuel Akintola (later premier of Western Nigeria) Kwame Nkruma (who formed the first African government in black Africa in 1951), and Jomo Kenyatta (President of Kenya).

As the African nations achieved independence, Pan-Africanism remained an ideal, and Du Bois continued to be influential. After he renounced his American citizenship he settled in Ghana on the invitation of President Nkruma and began work on his *Encyclopedia Africana*. At the age of ninety-three, after fighting for equal rights for the Negro for over half a century, Du Bois joined the Communist party, and at ninety-four, on August 27, 1963, he died in his cottage in Ghana.

Du Bois's disillusionment is as much an American tragedy as is the alienation of many black Americans today. For more than three hundred years, America has discriminated against her black citizens, and now is paying the price. As Du Bois wrote in *The Souls of Black Folk*, "We have no right to sit silently by while the inevitable seeds are sown for a harvest of disaster to our children, black and white."

Bibliography

ADAMS, RUSSELL. *Great Negroes Past and Present*. Chicago: Afro-Am Publishing Company, 1965.

ALEXANDER, MICHAEL. *Nine Who Helped Make America Great*. New York: Birk & Co., 1968.

APTHEKER, HERBERT. *A Documentary History of the Negro People in the United States,* Vol. II. New York: Citadel Press, 1951.

BECKWOURTH, JAMES. *The Life and Adventures of James Beckwourth*. New York: Arno Press and New York Times, 1969.

BENNETT, LERONE JR. *Before the Mayflower. A History of Black America*. Chicago: Johnson Publishing Co., 1962, 1969.

BONTEMPS, ARNA, ed. *Negro American Heritage*. San Francisco: Century Schoolbook Press, 1966.

BONTEMPS, ARNA. *Story of the Negro*. New York: Alfred A. Knopf, 1964.

BRAGG, REV. GEORGE F., JR., D.D. *Men of Maryland*. Baltimore: Advocate Press, 1925.

BRAWLEY, BENJAMIN. *Negro Builders and Heroes*. Chapel Hill: University of North Carolina Press, 1937.

CLAYTON, EDWARD. *The Negro Politician*. Chicago: Johnson Publishing Co., 1964.

DAVIDSON, BASIL. *African Kingdoms*. Morristown, N.J.: Silver Burdett, 1966.

_____. *The African Past*. New York: Grossett and Dunlap, 1967.

_____. *A History of West Africa to the Nineteenth Century*. Garden City: Anchor Books, Doubleday and Co., 1966.

_____. *Which Way Africa?* Baltimore: Penguin Books, 1967.

DAVIS, JOHN, ed. *American Negro Reference Book*. Englewood Cliffs: Prentice-Hall, 1966.

DOBLER, LAVINIA and WILLIAM BROWN. *Great Rulers of the African Past*. New York: Doubleday and Co., 1965.

DOREN, CHARLES, ed. *The Negro in American History*. New York: Encyclopedia Britannica, 1969.

DOUGLASS, FREDERICK. *Life and Times of Frederick Douglass*. New York: Macmillan, 1962.

DU BOIS, W. E. B. *Dusk of Dawn: An Essay Toward an Autobiography of a Race Concept*. New York: Schocken Books, 1968.

_____. *Souls of Black Folk*. New York: Fawcett Publications, 1964.

DURHAM, PHILIP. *The Negro Cowboys*. New York: Dodd Mead and Co., 1965.

EBONY EDITORS. *Ebony Pictorial History of Black America, Vol. I*. Chicago: Johnson Publishing Co., 1971.

FELTON, HAROLD. *Jim Beckwourth,* Negro Mountain Man. New York: Dodd, Mead and Co., 1966.

FRANKLIN, JOHN. *From Slavery to Freedom.* New York: Vintage Books, 1969.

GRAHAM, SHIRLEY. *Your Most Humble Servant: Benjamin Banneker.* New York: Messner, 1949.

GRANT, JOANNE, ed. *Black Protest: History, Documents and Analyses 1619 to the Present.* Greenwich: Fawcett Publications, 1968.

GREENE, ROBERT EWELL. *Black Defenders of America 1775-1973.* Chicago: Johnson Publishing Co., 1974.

HARDWICK, RICHARD. *Charles R. Drew.* New York: Charles Scribners Sons, 1967.

HERRING, HUBERT. *A History of Latin America.* New York: Alfred Knopf, 1968.

HOLT, SOL. *World Geography and You.* New Jersey: Van Nostrand, 1964.

HUGHES, LANGSTON and MILTON MELTZER. *A Pictorial History of the Negro in America.* New York: Crown Publishers, Inc., 1963.

KAPLAN, SIDNEY. *The Black Presence in the Era of the American Revolution 1770-1800.* Washington, D.C.: New York Graphic Society in Association with the Smithsonian Institution Press, 1973.

KATZ, WILLIAM. *Eyewitness: The Negro in American History.* New York: Pitman Publishing Corp., 1968.

LECKIE, WILLIAM. *The Buffalo Soldiers.* University of Oklahoma Press, 1967.

LEE, IRVIN. *Negro Medal of Honor Winners.* New York: Dodd, Mead and Co., 1967.

LINCOLN, ERIC. *The Negro Pilgrimage in America.* New York: Bantam Books, 1967.

LOGAN, RAYFORD. *The Negro in American Life and Thought, the Nadir: 1877-1901.* New York: Collier Macmillan, 1965.

McPHERSON, JAMES. *The Negro's Civil War.* New York: Pantheon Books, 1965.

MARKHAM, CLEMENTS. *Historia del Peru.* Lima: 1952.

MEIER, AUGUST. *Negro Thought in America, 1880-1915.* Ann Arbor: University of Michigan Press, 1964.

MELTZER, MILTON. *In Their Own Words: A History of the American Negro.* New York: T. Y. Crowell, 1964.

MILLER, FLOYD. *Ahdoolo: The Biography of Matthew A. Henson.* New York: Dutton, 1963.

MORAIS, HERBERT. *The History of the Negro in Medicine* (International Library of Negro Life and History series). New York: Publishers Co. Inc., 1968.

REDDING, SAUNDERS. *The Lonesome Road.* New York: Doubleday and Co., 1958.

ROBINSON, WILHELMINA. *Historical Negro Biographies* (International Library of Negro Life and History series). New York: Publishers Co. Inc., 1968.

ROLLINS, CHARLEMAE and BENJAMIN QUARLES. *Lift Every Voice.* New York: Doubleday, 1965.

ROLLINS, CHARLEMAE. *They Showed the Way.* New York: T. Y. Crowell, 1964.

SIMMONS, WILLIAM J. *Men of Mark.* Chicago: Johnson Publishing Co., 1970.

STAMPP, KENNETH. *The Peculiar Institution.* New York: Alfred Knopf, 1956.

STERLING, PHILIP and RAYFORD LOGAN. *Four Took Freedom*. New York: Doubleday, 1965.

WALKER, DAVID. *Appeal to the Colored Citizens of the World*. New York: Arno Press and New York Times, 1969.

WELLS-BARNETT, IDA. *On Lynchings: Southern Horror, A Red Record, Mob Rule in New Orleans*. New York: Arno Press and New York Times, 1969.

WIEDNER, DONALD. *A History of Africa South of the Sahara*. New York: Vintage Books, 1962.

WISH, HARVEY, editor. *The Negro Since Emancipation*. New Jersey: Prentice-Hall, 1964.

WOODSON, CARTER. *The Story of the Negro Retold*. Washington: Associated Publishers, 1969.

Index